JUN - 5 2015

ORCHID

MANTISES

AND OTHER *EXTREME* INSECT ADAPTATIONS

by Jodi Wheeler-Toppen

Consultant:
Robert T. Mason
Professor of Integrative Biology
Oregon State University
Cornvallis, Oregon

CAPSTONE PRESS
a capstone imprint

Fact Finders Books are published by Capstone Press,
1710 Roe Crest Drive, North Mankato, Minnesota 56003
www.capstonepub.com

Library of Congress Cataloging-in-Publication Data
Wheeler-Toppen, Jodi, author.
  Orchid mantises and other extreme insect adaptations / by Jodi Wheeler-Toppen, PhD.
    pages cm. — (Fact finders. Extreme adaptations)
  Summary: "Explores various extreme insect adaptations throughout the world, including meganosed flies, assassin bugs, and bombardier beetles"—Provided by publisher.
  Audience: Ages 8-10.
  Audience: Grades 4 to 6.
  Includes bibliographical references and index.
  ISBN 978-1-4914-0166-8 (library binding)
  ISBN 978-1-4914-0171-2 (paperback)
  ISBN 978-1-4914-0175-0 (ebook pdf)
1. Insects—Adaptation—Juvenile literature. 2. Insects—Physiology—Juvenile literature. 3. Adaptation (Biology)—Juvenile literature. I. Title.
  QL495.W44 2015
  595.714—dc23   2014006950

Developed and Produced by Focus Strategic Communications, Inc.
  Adrianna Edwards: project manager
  Ron Edwards, Jessica Pegis: editors
  Rob Scanlan: designer and compositor
  Diane Hartmann: media researcher
  Francine Geraci: copy editor and proofreader
  Wendy Scavuzzo: fact checker

Photo Credits
Alamy: Universal Images Group Limited, 7; Glow Images/Tips RM/Francesco Tomasinelli, cover, 1, iStock: fz750, 21, Wirepec, 17; Shutterstock: Andrey Pavlov, 29, Dr. Morley Read, 19, Evgeniy Ayupov, 9, Frank L Junior, 28, Henrik Larsson, 26, johannviloria, 25, Jordan Lye, 15, kamnuan, 8, Katarina Christenson, 22, Marco Uliana, 14, Matt Knoth, 27, Miroslav Fechtner, 6, Pawel Kielpinski, 20, Robert Biedermann, 24 (left), Sari Oneal, 12, Sherjaca, 16 (bottom), siloto, 24 (right); Thinkstock: FourOaks, 16 (top), ivkuzmin, 23, JupiterImages, 13, Péter Gudella, 18, PrinPrince, 4; Wikipedia: Bugboy52.40, 10, 11, GermanOle, 5

Design Elements
Shutterstock: Gordan, Osvath Zsolt

Printed in the United States of America in Stevens Point, Wisconsin.
032014   008092WZF14

TABLE OF CONTENTS

CHAPTER ONE

EXTREME INSECTS

Malaysia has exploding ants. French Guiana is home to a beetle that is bigger than your hand. New Zealand has a fly that makes webs like a spider. And in the United States, watch out for giant water beetles. They can suck the insides out of a toad, leaving its skin like a deflated balloon.

THE STAG BEETLE—ANOTHER EXTREME INSECT! SOME PEOPLE KEEP THEM AS PETS. MALE STAG BEETLES USE THEIR HUGE JAWS TO FIGHT EACH OTHER.

Each of these surprising traits is an adaptation. An adaptation is a change that allows an insect to live in a new place, eat a new food, or escape from its enemies in a new way.

AIRBORNE GIANT

Imagine you are walking outside and feel a shadow overhead. You look up and see a dragonfly-like creature the size of a duck. From below, you can see sharp jaws and the spines on its front legs. These body parts keep its food from wiggling away. It speeds past you and snatches a giant roach off the ground. Fossils show that just such an insect, called the griffenfly, lived around Kansas and Oklahoma more than 250 million years ago. No humans were around to see them, and modern insects are smaller.

A MODEL OF THE ENORMOUS GRIFFENFLY, WHICH LIVED 250 MILLION YEARS AGO

CHAPTER TWO

A BUG'S LIFE

The standard insect body is divided into three segments. Each segment has bendable parts that stick out. Scientists call these parts **jointed appendages**.

The whole body is wrapped in an **exoskeleton**. This is a crunchy skin that also does the job of bones. If you were to crack open a dragonfly, you wouldn't find a single bone. Instead, the exoskeleton gives an insect its shape and provides a place for muscles to attach.

joint—a place where a body part bends

appendage—a limb or other part that sticks out of an animal or plant

exoskeleton—a structure on the outside of an animal that gives it support

DRAGONFLY

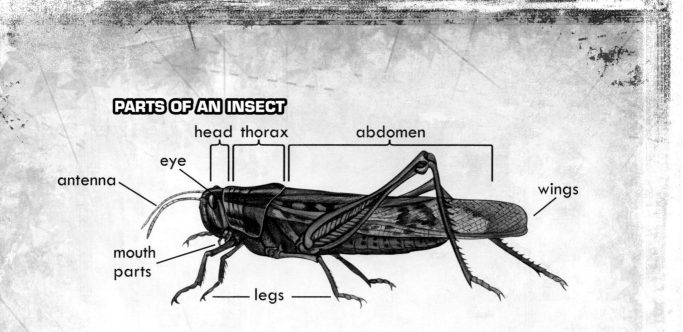

PARTS OF AN INSECT

head thorax abdomen

eye

antenna

wings

mouth
parts

legs

MILLIONS OF INSECTS

The basic insect body plan has room for all of its adaptations. There are more **species** of insects than any other living thing. So far, scientists have found more than a million different kinds. They suspect there are as many as three million species still to be discovered. Some of these millions have developed extreme adaptations.

species—a group of plants or animals that share common characteristics

GROWING UP GLOWING

Young lightning bugs are nothing like the fireflies you may have seen in the summer sky. They can't fly. They look like tiny alligators. They crawl across the forest floor and suck the guts out of snails, slugs, and worms. But the youngsters do have the coolest adaptation of the lightning bug: they glow. Their eerie light is a warning to spiders and toads that they are poisonous.

A BABY LIGHTNING BUG

AMAZING ADOLESCENTS

Some young insects look like little adults. They live in the same places and eat the same food as adults. This way of growing up is called incomplete **metamorphosis**. Young insects that go through incomplete metamorphosis are called **nymphs**.

BABY PRAYING MANTISES LOOK VERY SIMILAR TO THE ADULTS. PRAYING MANTISES GO THROUGH INCOMPLETE METAMORPHOSIS.

metamorphosis—changing from one form into a very different form, like a caterpillar to a butterfly

nymph—a young form of an insect; nymphs change into adults by shedding their skin many times

Other young insects, such as lightning bugs, do not look like the adults. They live in different places and eat different foods. This way of growing up is called complete metamorphosis. In complete metamorphosis, the young insect is called a **larva**.

Complete metamorphosis is an important insect adaptation. It means that the adults and larvae do not have to compete against each other to find food.

larva—an insect at the stage of development between an egg and an adult; larvae is plural for larva

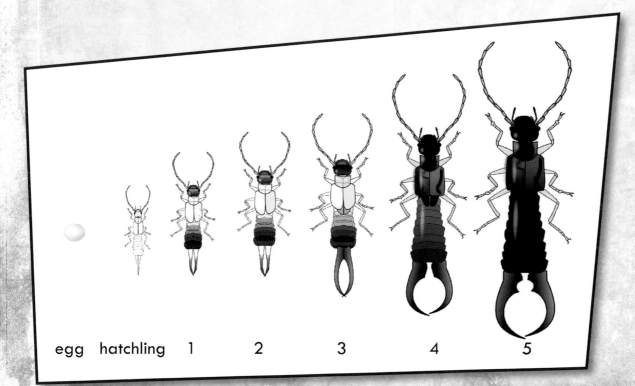

egg   hatchling   1   2   3   4   5

AN EARWIG GOES THROUGH INCOMPLETE METAMORPHOSIS. IT GROWS BIGGER AND BIGGER UNTIL IT IS AN ADULT.

METAMORPHO-MAGGOT

Drone fly larvae are so different from adult drone flies that they even have a different name—rat-tailed maggots. Drone flies collect nectar from flowers. Rat-tailed maggots prefer to eat rotting meat and sewage. They live in sewer water and on wet, dead animals. Their name comes from a long, thin tube that they stick out of the gunk, like a snorkel, so they can breathe.

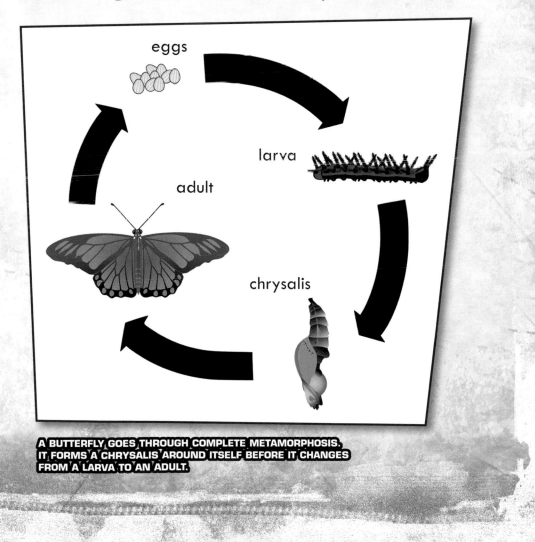

eggs

larva

adult

chrysalis

A BUTTERFLY GOES THROUGH COMPLETE METAMORPHOSIS. IT FORMS A CHRYSALIS AROUND ITSELF BEFORE IT CHANGES FROM A LARVA TO AN ADULT.

CHAPTER THREE

SURPRISING SUPPERS

In the jungles of southern Africa, a meganosed fly slides its 4-inch (10-centimeter) mouth into a flower. Its mouth is shaped like a straw. The fly uses it to drink nectar from thin, deep flowers. Four inches may seem small, but it's five times longer than the fly's body. That would be like you dragging a 25-foot (7.6-meter) straw everywhere! And meganosed flies aren't alone. In Madagascar the Morgan's sphinx moth has a 12-inch (30-cm) tongue. This tongue is easy to manage. It can be rolled up when not in use.

A MORGAN'S SPHINX MOTH DRINKS THE NECTAR OF A PETUNIA.

MIGHTY MOUTH

The earliest insects had mouths that chewed. Crickets, grasshoppers, roaches, beetles, and praying mantises still munch their food. But eating got more interesting when insects grew mouth parts that let them drink their food.

SUCKER

The giant water bug lives in North America, Europe, and Asia. Its needle-like mouth parts let it pierce the skin of an animal much bigger than itself. It can pierce a fish, toad, or baby turtle. It injects the animal with digestive juices that turn the animal's insides to mush. Then the water bug sucks up its meal. Only the skin is left behind.

THE GIANT WATER BUG IS ABLE TO CATCH FISH AND OTHER SMALL ANIMALS.

A VAMPIRE'S VAMPIRE

One bug can beat the vampire bat at its own game—bloodsucking. Assassin bugs found in Central America stick their sucking mouth parts into sleeping bats. Then they drink their fill of rich, delicious bat-blood!

THE ASSASSIN BUG OF CENTRAL AMERICA

SLIME LOVER

Blowflies have a different set of adaptations for drinking. Their mouths are more like a sponge. And the liquid they love? Slimy, soupy rotting animals. The flies land on dead bodies and run their mouths across the surface to absorb the decaying meat.

BLOWFLIES ALSO BLOW BUBBLES. SCIENTISTS THINK THEY MAY BE CLEANING THEIR MOUTH PARTS.

FACT

Blowflies can provide helpful clues at a crime scene. Crime scene investigators (CSIs) can look at the types of blowflies on a body to figure out how long the person has been dead.

SUPPER IS WHAT?

Some insects are adapted to eat poop. That's because poop has calories, or energy. When food is digested, some undigested parts are passed that are still good to eat. Dung beetles gather up poop, roll it in a ball, and bury it. Then they lay eggs on the poop. When the eggs hatch, the larvae dig into the feast.

ONCE THE DUNG BEETLE HAS ROLLED UP ITS BALL OF POOP, IT BURIES IT.

A POOPY PROBLEM

Different types of dung beetles are adapted to different kinds of poop. In Australia the dung beetles ate kangaroo dung. When cows were brought to the country, the dung beetles did not like the larger cow dumps. Cow poop piled up everywhere! Scientists in Australia had to bring in dung beetles that were adapted to eating cow pies. These beetles, which had more babies and were better at eating leftover grass, were able to take care of the mess.

AN AUSTRALIAN MOTHER COW AND CALF

DINNER IS DEAD

The American burying beetle collects dead animals for its young. The male and female beetles dig a hole for a small corpse. Then they strip off the fur or feathers. The parents chew up the meat for their youngest larvae.

The bodies of these beetles are adapted for this lifestyle. Their legs are shaped for digging. Their sharp mouth parts help them slice off the skin. They even produce a liquid antibiotic to spread on the dead body and slow down decay.

AMERICAN BURYING BEETLES

SHALL I HAVE YOU FOR DINNER?

Botflies latch onto their meals. Human botfly larvae live in Central and South America. They develop inside the skin of an unlucky person. They release digestive juices and then absorb the tissue. To protect against human fingers, the larvae have sharp hooks. If the victim tries to pull the larvae out, they just dig in tighter.

THE ADULT HUMAN BOTFLY

DEADLY PASSENGERS

Parasitoid wasps also go in for live meat. The backside of a female parasitoid wasp looks like a stinger. But it is really an adaptation for laying eggs inside a **host** such as caterpillars. The eggs hatch and slowly eat the living caterpillar over several days or weeks.

host—an animal from which another animal gets nutrition

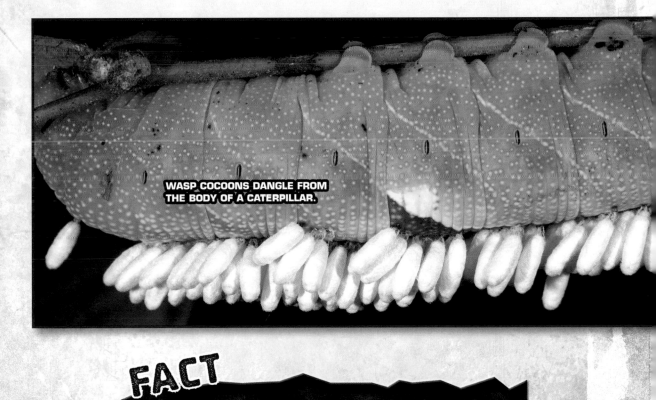

WASP COCOONS DANGLE FROM THE BODY OF A CATERPILLAR.

FACT

Even parasitoid wasp larvae have to watch out. There are parasitoids that live only in other parasitoid larvae! Only the inside larvae will survive.

CHAPTER FOUR

ON THE HUNT

Some insect predators chase down their **prey**. But this takes a lot of energy. Through adaptation these insects have developed ways to trick their food into coming to them.

FLOWER FAKE OUT

See that beautiful pink and purple flower? A fly buzzes down to sample the nectar. But it's not a flower! It's a hungry Malaysian orchid mantis.

prey—an animal hunted by another animal for food

THE BEAUTIFUL ORCHID MANTIS ATTRACTS INSECTS BY FAKING IT AS A FLOWER.

A PRAYING MANTIS TRAPS A MOTH.

FATAL LIGHT

The larvae of the New Zealand glowworm live in caves. They produce clear, sticky threads that dangle from the ceiling like spider webs. The larvae glow, and other insects are drawn to the light. Once the insects get tangled in the threads, they become a larvae snack.

THE ASSASSIN'S GAME

Stenolemus assassin bugs take on spiders at their own game. They can creep across webs without getting stuck. They time their movements to match gusts of wind. That way, the spiders don't feel the web jiggling.

predator—an animal that kills and eats other animals

FACT

One type of assassin bug eats ants and then glues the ant body on its back. This bug avoids jumping spiders, which are its **predator**. However, the jumping spiders don't recognize the assassin bug with its ant body.

AN ASSASSIN BUG PRETENDS TO BE AN ANT BY PLACING THE ANT'S BODY ON ITS BACK.

HOW I LOVE … TO EAT YOU

Fireflies use their lights to call for mates. Each type of firefly has its own flash pattern. When a male flashes for a female, he knows that the right kind of female is answering. However, some females know a foreign language. They copy the flash patterns of other types of fireflies. When a male shows up to mate, she eats him.

A FIREFLY IN FLIGHT

NOT SO FAST, BUSTER

Predators aren't the only bugs with tricks. As soon as a predator develops new tactics, its prey begin to adapt and find ways to avoid being eaten.

IN THE HOT SEAT

Japanese honeybees have a vicious enemy—Asian giant hornets. In just minutes these hornets can take over a beehive and slice the heads off every bee in the colony. The hornet's shell is too thick for the honeybee's stinger. So the bees mob the hornet and heat their bodies until the hornet cooks to death.

JAPANESE HONEYBEE

ASIAN GIANT HORNET

REAR GUARD

When a bombardier beetle is in danger, it fires boiling hot acid out of its rear end. The tip of its abdomen can move, so it can aim the spray right at its attacker.

POOP DEFENSE

Would you smear yourself in poop to stay safe? Three-lined potato beetle larvae do. They eat plants, such as deadly nightshade, that contain poisons. The poisons don't bother them, though. They just pass it out of their body as waste. The larvae let the waste collect all over their back. Nothing says "don't eat me" like poisoned poop!

THE BOMBARDIER BEETLE SPRAYS ITS ENEMIES WITH ACID TO PROTECT ITSELF.

YOU'RE THE BOMB

Malaysian carpenter ants explode to protect their nest-mates. These ants store toxic, sticky glue in glands inside their heads. When an enemy approaches, a worker ant moves in and blows up, killing both of them. While this adaptation kills the worker ant, it benefits the rest of the colony.

THE MALAYSIAN CARPENTER ANT BLOWS ITSELF UP WHEN ITS NEST-MATES ARE THREATENED.

MASTER OF DISGUISES

Asian swallowtail caterpillars start out life looking like a bird's least favorite food—bird poop! However, as they grow, they begin to look like the leaf they live on. If these two tricks don't work, this insect sprouts bright orange horns if a predator approaches. These "horns" are actually glands on the caterpillar's head. The look is scary, and the glands also smell and taste awful!

STAY AWAY! THE ASIAN SWALLOWTAIL CATERPILLAR SPROUTS HORNS WHEN A PREDATOR APPROACHES.

CHAPTER FIVE

INVASION OF THE INSECTS

Insects are built for adapting to new places. Most insects fly, so they can travel to new homes. They are small, so they don't need much room when they get there. And insects have lots of babies. With each baby, there is a chance for a new adaptation to give them an advantage in their new home.

A SPIDER WITH
HER TINY BABIES

INSECTS TAKE ON THE WORLD

You can find insects in extreme habitats all over the world. Chironomid live in Antarctica. They are adapted to survive freezing temperatures. They can go without oxygen for weeks. They can also tolerate huge amounts of salt.

Saharan desert ants can survive temperatures of 140°F (60°C). Their extra-long legs lift them above the hot sand. There are oil flies that live in toxic oil spills, diving beetles that can stay underwater for hours, and midges that can dry out completely and spring back to life when it rains.

If there is a new habitat or a new way to live, you can bet some kind of insect will find a way to adapt to the new environment.

A SAHARAN DESERT ANT HOLDS A DEAD MIDGE.

GLOSSARY

appendage (uh-PEN-dij)—a limb or other part that sticks out of an animal or plant

exoskeleton (ek-soh-SKE-luh-tuhn)—a structure on the outside of an animal that gives it support

host (HOHST)—an animal from which another animal gets nutrition

joint (JOINT)—a place where two parts meet

larva (LAR-vuh)—an insect at the stage of development between an egg and an adult; larvae is plural for larva

metamorphosis (meht-uh-MOR-fuh-siss)—changing from one form into a very different form, like a caterpillar to a butterfly

nymph (NIMF)—a young form of an insect; nymphs change into adults by shedding their skin many times

predator (PRED-uh-tur)—an animal that hunts other animals for food

prey (PRAY)—an animal hunted by another animal for food

species (SPEE-shiez)—a group of plants or animals that share common characteristics

READ MORE

Heos, Bridget. *What to Expect When You are Expecting Larvae*. Expecting Animal Babies. Minneapolis, Minn.: MillBrook Press, 2011.

Jenkins, Steve. *The Beetle Book*. Boston: Houghton Mifflin, 2012.

Rake, Jody Sullivan. *Why Bedbugs Bite and Other Gross Facts About Bugs*. Gross Me Out. Mankato, Minn.: Capstone Press, 2012.

Shea, Nicole. *Creepy Bugs*. Nature's Creepiest Creatures. New York: Gareth Stevens, 2012.

CRITICAL THINKING
USING THE COMMON CORE

1. Reread pages 6–7. List three important pieces of information in these pages pertaining to insect body parts and adaptations. Decide which body part is the most important and explain why. Use examples from the text to support your opinion. (Key Ideas and Details)

2. Use text features to find information about insects that eat poop. What text features did you use? How did they help you find the information quickly? (Craft and Structure)

3. Reread pages 20–23. Pick two of the insects. Explain how they are the same and different. Use information from the text and online research to support your answer. If you were an insect scientist, which one would you study? Why? Include examples from the words and pictures to explain your thinking. (Integration of Knowledge and Ideas)

INTERNET SITES

FactHound offers a safe, fun way to find Internet sites related to this book. All of the sites on FactHound have been researched by our staff.

Here's all you do:

Visit *www.facthound.com*

Type in this code: 9781491401668

 Check out projects, games, and lots more at **www.capstonekids.com**

INDEX